ᵀᴴᴱKIDS' WORLD ALMANAC®
Rhyming Dictionary

™KIDS' WORLD ALMANAC®
Rhyming Dictionary
A Guide for
Young Poets and Songwriters

Peter Israel and Peg Streep

Illustrated by Heidi Stetson

WORLD ALMANAC
AN IMPRINT OF PHAROS BOOKS • A SCRIPPS HOWARD COMPANY
NEW YORK

First published in 1991.

Library of Congress Cataloging-in-Publication Data

Israel, Peter
    The kids' World Almanac rhyming dictionary ; a guide for young poets and songwriters / Peter Israel and Peg Streep : illustrated by Heidi Stetson.
        p.   cm.
    Includes index.
    Summary: A rhyming dictionary organized by phonetic word endings in alphabetical order.
    ISBN 0-88687-576-5 (hardcover) : $12.95
    1. English language—Rhyme—Dictionaries, Juvenile.
[1. English language—Rhyme—Dictionaries.]   I. Streep, Peg.
II. Stetson, Heidi, ill.   III. Title.
PE1519.I8   1991
423'.1—dc20   90-42407
                                                        CIP
                                                         AC

Printed in the United States of America

World Almanac
An Imprint of Pharos Books
A Scripps Howard Company
200 Park Avenue
New York, NY 10166

10 9 8 7 6 5 4 3 2 1

Cover and interior design by Bea Jackson.
Cover and interior illustrations by Heidi Stetson.

for Alexandra
from her parents

Contents

How to Use This Book

One of the great things about writing songs and poems in English is that there are so many rhymes!

Our rhyming dictionary won't begin to give you all of them, not even half. Books that try to—and there are some—have many more pages and contain thousands of words, many of them difficult. What we have tried to do is to give you a head start, as a songwriter and poet, by including a wide variety of the simplest rhymes.

The best way to use this book is to use the Index at the back. Find the ending of the word you want to find rhymes for, then go to the page number next to it.

For example, suppose you want to find rhymes for *bread*. Look up **-ead** in the Index and go to the page next to it. You will find a list of other rhyming words ending in **-ead** (like *dead* and *spread*) but also words ending in **-ed** (like *bed* and *red*).

If you can't find your ending in the Index, chances are you're out of luck because we didn't include it; there probably weren't enough rhymes to go along with it. If this happens, you'll either have to look in an adult rhyming dictionary or find your own rhymes in your own vocabulary—which is a lot more fun.

You'll probably have the most fun of all if you add words to our rhyme lists and start your own pages for rhyme endings we've had to leave out.

We have also included lists of "Some harder words" to tempt you as a poet, and also some "Timely tips," "Quick quizzes" and a few "Be carefuls!" One of the tricky things about English is that many words *look* alike but don't *sound* alike.

The most important thing you can do, if you want rhymes which are exactly right, is to say words *aloud*.

The second most important thing you need to do, if you don't know what a word means, is to look it up! One of the key features of good poems and songs is that the words fit exactly in meaning as well as sound.

Finally, on many of the pages in this book, you will find sample poems, using rhymes listed on the page. Some of these are from other writers, and we've listed the authors when we know them. Many of them, though, we've written ourselves.

We hope they inspire you. We *know* you can do better!

Introduction

About Rhymes

The first poems written in English did not rhyme at all. Instead, they were made up of words that had the same *first* sounds, like this:

B*rown* b*irds,* b*ig* b*eaks*

or

L*ovely* l*adies,* l*ong* l*ashes*

or

P*eter* P*iper* p*icked a* p*eck of* p*ickled* p*eppers!*

The name for this is *alliteration.*
Rhyming came next.
No one knows who wrote the first rhyming song or poem, but you can bet that, whoever it was, he or she had fun. Rhyme depends on the *last* sound or sounds. A rhyme is two words (sometimes more) that sound the same at the end, like this:

A bird with a beak
Perched on the peak.

or

The bird with a beak
Wanted to speak.

or

Let's sing a song
All night long.

Rhymes can be used at the end of a line or in the middle. Watch this:

Said the tailor
To the sailor,
"You'd look cute
In a purple suit."

In this poem, the rhymes all come at the ends of the lines. But if you wanted to, you would write the same poem this way:

Said the tailor *to the* sailor,
"You'd look cute *in a purple* suit."

Done this way, the rhymes come within the lines, and the endings of the two lines no longer rhyme. But guess what? It's still a poem!

You can use rhymes almost any way you want. You can even use them in different ways within the same song or poem. You can have two lines rhyme, one right after the other, as the great writer, Robert Louis Stevenson, did in his poem "Foreign Lands:"

> *Up into the cherry* tree   (a)
> *Who should climb but little* me?   (a)
> *I held the trunk with both my* hands   (b)
> *And looked abroad on foreign* lands.   (b)

This is called an a-a-b-b rhyme scheme, because the first and second lines rhyme with each other, and then the third and the fourth lines rhyme with each other.

If you like, you can rhyme every other line instead, which is called an a-b-a-b rhyme scheme. Here's how Robert Louis Stevenson did it in his poem "The Swing:"

> *How do you like to go up in a* swing   (a)
> *Up in the air so* blue?   (b)
> *Oh, I do think it the pleasantest* thing   (a)
> *Ever a child can* do!   (b)

Notice that the first and third lines rhyme, then the second and the fourth lines rhyme.

If you're in the mood for something fancier, you can use different rhyming schemes within one poem. Here's Robert Louis Stevenson again, in a poem called "Windy Nights:"

> *Whenever the moon and stars are* set,   (a)
> *Whenever the wind is* high,   (b)
> *All night long in the dàrk and* wet   (a)
> *A man goes riding* by.   (b)
> *Late in the night, when the fires are* out, (c)
> *Why does he gallop and gallop* about?   (c)

The rhyme scheme here is the same a-b-a-b you've seen before (first line and third, second line and fourth), but the poet has added yet another new rhyme for the fifth and sixth lines. You can do this too. When the last two lines of a poem rhyme together, they are called a *couplet*.

There are also poems where only *some* of the lines rhyme. (There are even poems without *any* rhymes, but that's a very complicated subject!) Using lines that don't rhyme usually works best with a poem that is four lines or longer. Here's part of a poem called "The Brown Owl," by the poet who called herself Aunt Effie, that uses some rhyming lines and some that don't rhyme:

> *The brown owl sits in the ivy bush,*
> *And she looketh wondrous* wise,
> *With a horny beak beneath her cowl,*
> *And a pair of large round* eyes.

When you begin to write your songs and poems, you'll have to decide where you want your rhymes to go. You'll have lots of choices.

What Makes a Poem?

Rhyme is only part of what can make a song or poem. After all, when you're speaking to someone, or writing a letter, you might accidentally make a rhyme, but you're not making up poetry! For instance, you might say to someone, "I spent the whole day in the subway." *Day* and *subway* do rhyme, but is that a poem? Hardly. By the way, the word we use to describe writing that isn't poetry is *prose*.

Another equally important part of what makes a song or a poem is *beat* or *rhythm*, sometimes called *meter*.

You'll need to tap or drum in order to learn about rhythm. A pencil is an easy thing to use, or even your foot on the floor, or the palm of your hand on a table.

Begin by saying the words out loud. Ready?

Start by saying this poem aloud:

> *One, two,*
> *Buckle my shoe.*
> *Three, four,*
> *Open the door.*

Now, tap or drum every time you make a new sound. It should sound like this:

> *Dum Dum*
> *Dum-dum Dum Dum*
> *Dum Dum*
> *Dum-dum Dum Dum.*

The word "One" gets one Dum. So do all the other words which have only *one* sound. But "Buckle" and "Open" get two Dums each. Can you guess why that is? It's because they each have *two* sounds:

> Buck-*le*
> O-*pen*

In case you didn't know, each of the sounds in a word is called a *syllable*. "Shoe" is a one-syllable word;

"buckle" is a two-syllable word. You can always tell by saying the word out loud and counting the sounds. (How many syllables does "syllable" have?)

Okay, let's try a harder one. Begin by saying this poem out loud:

> *Mary had a little lamb.*
> *Her fleece was white as snow.*
> *And everywhere that Mary went,*
> *The lamb was sure to go.*

Now, tap or drum every time you make a new sound. It should go like this:

> *Dum-dum Dum Dum Dum-dum Dum*
> *Dum Dum Dum Dum Dum Dum*
> *Dum Dum-dum-Dum Dum Dum-dum Dum*
> *Dum Dum Dum Dum Dum Dum*

But wait a minute. Did you notice, when you tapped, that some of your taps were louder or stronger than others? Say the poem aloud again, tapping as you go, and listen for when the sound in the word is important. It should go like this:

> *Mary had a little lamb,*
> *DUM-dum DUM dum DUM-dum DUM*
> *Her fleece was white as snow.*
> *Dum DUM dum DUM dum DUM*
> *And everywhere that Mary went,*
> *Dum DUM-dum-DUM dum DUM-dum DUM*
> *The lamb was sure to go.*
> *Dum DUM dum DUM dum DUM.*

It's no accident that the first line and third line have the same number of heavier beats, or "DUMS," in almost the same position and order, and that the second line and fourth line are absolutely the same, when it comes to little "dums" and big "DUMS."

If you want to test for yourself how important rhythm is, just suppose Mary *didn't* have a little lamb, but an elephant instead! That means that the poem would have to read like this:

> *Mary had a little elephant,*
> *Her fleece was white as snow.*
> *And everywhere that Mary went,*
> *The elephant was sure to go.*

Try saying it out loud now! It's not as easy, because now the rhythm doesn't work. It's very important for the poem that Mary have a *lamb* (which has only one syllable) and not an *elephant* (which has three syllables).

And if you think *elephant* is bad, try "Mary Had a Little Lamb" with a *hippopotamus*! (Hippopotamus has five syllables.)

All poems are made up of big "DUMS" and little "dums." They are called *stressed* syllables or sounds (for the important ones) and *unstressed* syllables or sounds (for the minor ones). They're there even if you haven't planned for them, and that's because, when we speak English, we pronounce words in a certain way.

A poet or songwriter has to pay extra-special attention to beat and rhythm.

Why Write Songs and Poems?

People write songs and poems for the same reason they play games: because it's *fun*!

And let's get one thing straight: A song is simply a poem set to music. You can see this for yourself by writing out the words to a song for yourself. Take the first chorus of the famous song, "America The Beautiful," for example:

> *America, America,*
> *God shed His grace on thee,*
> *And crown thy good*
> *With brotherhood,*
> *From sea to shining sea.*

If you check for rhymes and rhythm, you will find both, just as in a poem, and you can do the same for any song.

Sometimes, a song or poem begins with an idea. Sometimes it begins with a picture the writer has in mind. Here's a poem by Sara Teasdale that really is like a picture. It's called "The Falling Star:"

> *I saw a star slide down the sky,*
> *Blinding the north as it went by,*
> *Too lovely to be bought or sold,*
> *Too burning and too quick to hold,*
> *Good only to make wishes on,*
> *And then forever to be gone.*

Can you see the falling star she describes? Doesn't it remind you of stars *you've* seen at night?

Poets also write poems just to be funny or silly. Here's one, by Gelett Burgess, that's for fun:

> *I never saw a purple cow,*
> *I never hope to see one;*
> *But I can tell you anyhow,*
> *I'd rather see than be one.*

And here's one that's quite silly:

> *There was a young girl whose nose*
> *Reached practically down to her toes.*
> *She sniffed and she sneezed,*
> *She chortled and wheezed,*
> *Whenever she smelled a red rose.*

This last poem, by the way, is called a *limerick*. A limerick is a special kind of poem which has five lines, a rollicking rhythm, and an a-a-b-b-a rhyme scheme. The most famous limerick writer was Edward Lear. Limericks are great fun to make up, and you should certainly try some.

There are many other kinds of poems, and over the centuries, rules for each kind have come into being. One of the oldest, the *ballad*, started out as a song. At first, ballads weren't even written down but were taught by parents to their children and passed on. Often a ballad tells a dramatic story. It usually has repeating lines, called a *refrain*. The following famous ballad, "Greensleeves," was first sung in the 15th century (over 500 years ago!) and was popular during Shakespeare's time, in the 16th century:

Greensleeves was all my joy,
Greensleeves was my delight,
Greensleeves was my heart of gold,
And who but Lady Greensleeves.

Alas, my love, ye do me wrong,
To cast me off discourteously.
And I have loved you so long,
Delighting in your company.

Greensleeves was all my joy,
Greensleeves was my delight,
Greensleeves was my heart of gold,
And who but Lady Greensleeves.

I have been ready at your hand,
To grant whatever you would crave,
I have both waged life and land,
Your love and good will for to have.

Greensleeves was all my joy,
Greensleeves was my delight,
Greensleeves was my heart of gold,
And who but Lady Greensleeves.

The music for "Greensleeves" is still well known today and has been recorded many times. If you don't already know it, ask your parents or your teacher to sing or play it for you!

A ballad is a popular poem, told in plain language. Most other types of rhyming poems are more formal, following very strict rules. The *sonnet*, for instance, first made famous by Shakespeare and the poet Petrarch, is always fourteen lines long. It is written in lines that have exactly ten beats and follows a very particular rhyme scheme.

There are also kinds of poems without rhymes. *Free verse* and *blank verse* are two of them. *Haiku*, which came originally from the Zen religion in Japan, are miniature poems without rhymes. They are interesting to read, extremely hard to write. Even *rap* is a kind of spoken poetry, although it concentrates a lot more on beat than it does on rhymes or meaning. In our opinion, though, you shouldn't tackle the rhymeless forms of poetry until you know how to use rhymes.

Probably the most important thing about songs and poems is that they express things that are inside you. They can be happy or sad, just as you are sometimes happy and sometimes sad. They can be serious or silly. They can describe real things—things you see and hear—or imaginary things that you only see inside. They can be very short or very long. They can rhyme in any number of ways, and there are many rhythms you can make up to match what you are feeling.

It's all up to you.

The Rhymes

–ab rhymes

blab	dab	grab	scab	stab
cab	drab	jab	slab	tab
crab	gab	nab		

*How to **grab***
*A moving **crab**?*
Sideways!

–able rhymes (also –abel)

able	fable	label	stable
cable	gable	sable	table

–ace rhymes (also –ase)

ace	case	face	mace	race
base	chase	grace	pace	space
brace	erase	lace	place	trace

Some harder words: deface, disgrace, displace, efface, embrace, misplace, replace, retrace, staircase, suitcase, unlace

Quick quiz: Some easy-looking words are really hard. Take mace, for instance. Do you know what it means? Actually, it has three meanings: a spice; a medieval weapon; a chemical spray.

*There once was a girl named **Grace**.*
*Who came from **Samothrace**.*
I'd like to go there,
But she won't tell me where,
*Though she said it's a marvelous **place**.*

–ack rhymes (also –ac; –ak)

attack	hack	quack	smack	track
back	jack	rack	snack	whack
black	knack	sack	stack	yak
clack	lack	shack	tack	
crack	pack	slack		

Some harder words: bric-à-brac, cognac, flapjack, flashback, fullback, halfback, hijack, horseback, hunchback, kayak, knapsack, knick-knack, lilac, lumberjack, ransack, setback, shellac, sumac, thumbtack, wisecrack

It's Jack and Jill,
The poem says,
But why not Jill and **Jack***?*
If Jill fell down
And broke her crown
And Jack came running **back***?*
I wonder why Jack must go first,
Why Jack it is who gets the worst.
Forget the question of their thirst.
So why not try another **tack***?*
Not Jack and Jill
But Jill and **Jack***?*

–act rhymes

act	extract	pact	tact
attract	fact	react	tract
exact	impact		

Some harder words: abstract, compact, contract, detract, distract, intact, retract, subtract

Timely tip: This rhyming list would be much longer if it included all the words which end in **–acked,** words like **backed**, **hacked**, **packed**, **tracked**, etc. Look back at the **–ack** rhyme page to find them.

–ad rhymes

ad	clad	gad	lad	sad
bad	dad	glad	mad	shad
cad	fad	had	pad	tad

Some harder words: brad, comrade, doodad, iron-clad, triad

–ade rhymes (also –aid; –ede)

ade	evade	laid	shade	suede
afraid	fade	maid	spade	wade
aid	glade	paid	staid	
blade	invade	parade	trade	
braid	jade	raid		

Some harder words: arcade, barricade, blockade, brigade, cascade, cavalcade, centigrade, charade, crusade, decade, degrade, escapade, grenade, inlaid, lemonade, marmalade, masquerade, mermaid, milkmaid, palisade, persuade, renegade, serenade, stockade, tirade

Timely tip: For still more rhymes, look up **–ay rhymes** for words to which you can add **–ed,** like **played**.

> *The Magic Mouse*
> *Wore shoes of **suede**.*
> *He built a house*
> *Of quartz and **jade**.*
> *And when you go there*
> *You will see*
> *The Magic Mouse's grand **parade**.*

–aff rhymes (also –affe; –alf; –aph; –augh)

calf   giraffe   half   staff
gaffe   graph   laugh

Some harder words: behalf, chaff, carafe, epitaph, monograph, paragraph, phonograph, photograph, telegraph

*"Mr. Photographer," said the **giraffe**,*
*"I hope this isn't a **gaffe**,*
*But please take another **photograph***
*That shows something more than my upper **half**."*
*"Why sure," he said with a belly **laugh**,*
*"I'll happily do it on your **behalf**."*

–aft rhymes

aft	daft	graft
craft	draft	shaft

Some harder words: aircraft, haft, handicraft, waft

Timely tip: Look under **–aff rhymes** for words to which you can add **–ed**—like **laughed**—which will make this skimpy list longer.

–ag rhymes

bag	flag	nag	shag	tag
brag	gag	rag	slag	wag
crag	hag	sag	snag	
drag	lag			

Some harder words: beanbag, carpetbag, dufflebag, handbag, saddlebag, sandbag, scallawag, wigwag, zigzag

–age rhymes (also –auge)

age	gauge	rage	wage
cage	page	sage	

Some harder words: enrage, outrage, rampage, upstage

Be careful! There are a great many words which end in **–age**—like **average**, **garbage**, **luggage**—but are not true rhymes to the words on this page because the ending is pronounced "**idge**." Please avoid them! When in doubt, say words out loud!

–ail rhymes (also –ale; –eil)

ail	female	kale	rail	tail
ale	flail	mail	sail	tale
bail	frail	male	sale	trail
bale	gale	nail	scale	veil
dale	hail	pail	shale	wail
detail	hale	pale	snail	whale
fail	jail	quail	stale	

Some harder words: assail, avail, bewail, blackmail, cocktail, curtail, exhale, grail, hangnail, impale, inhale, pigtail, prevail, retail, thumbnail, unveil, wholesale

*Over hill, over **dale**,*
*We will hit the dusty **trail**,*
As those caissons go rolling along.
—Edmund L. Gruber
("The Field Artillery Song")

–ain rhymes (also –agne; –ane; –eign; –ein)

bane	gain	pane	sane	vane
brain	grain	plain	stain	vein
cane	lane	plane	strain	wane
chain	main	rain	swain	
crane	mane	reign	vain	
drain	pain	rein		

Some harder words: abstain, airplane, campaign, champagne, complain, contain, deign, detain, disdain, entertain, explain, feign, humane, hurricane, insane, migraine, membrane, refrain, regain, restrain, retain, sustain, terrain, urbane

*There once was a happy old **crane**,*
*Who lived on a beach down in **Spain**.*
He swam in the sea,
Ate cookies, drank tea,
*But in secret he sipped dry **champagne**.*

–air rhymes (also –aire; –are; –ear; –eir; –ere)

air	fair	lair	snare	tear
bare	fare	mare	spare	their
bear	flair	pair	square	there
blare	flare	pare	stair	ware
care	hair	pear	stare	wear
chair	hare	rare	swear	where
dare	heir	scare		

Some harder words: affair, anywhere, aware, beware, compare, declare, éclair, fanfare, hardware, millionaire, nightmare, prepare, questionnaire, repair, solitaire, thoroughfare, underwear, unfair, welfare

*Take **care**
You don't **stare**
At a woolly **bear**
Who's taking the **air**
Outside his **lair**!*

–airy rhymes (also –ary)

airy	dairy	rosemary	vary
canary	fairy	unwary	wary
chary	hairy		

Some harder words: But there aren't any! Not really. Yes, there are all kinds of words that end in **–ary** and look as if they belong here, words like **adversary** and **voluntary**. But when you say them out loud, they sound like "**erry**," and that's where you'll have to look for them.

–ait rhymes (also –ate; –eight)

ate	eight	grate	plate	state
bait	fate	great	rate	straight
crate	freight	hate	skate	strait
create	gait	late	slate	wait
date	gate	mate	spate	weight

Some harder words: abate, aggravate, celebrate, debate, dictate, delegate, elevate, estate, frustrate, illustrate, irritate, magistrate, migrate, narrate, ornate, overrate, pate, penetrate, rebate, rotate, sate, sedate, translate, vibrate

–ake rhymes (also –ache; –aque; –eak)

ache	break	flake	pancake	stake
awake	cake	lake	quake	steak
bake	drake	make	rake	take
brake	fake	mistake	snake	wake

Some harder words: clambake, cornflake, daybreak, earthquake, forsake, handshake, headache, heartbreak, keepsake, kittiwake, mandrake, namesake, opaque, outbreak, overtake, rattlesnake, snowflake, sweepstake, undertake

Quick quiz: What's a **drake**? a **kittiwake**? a **mandrake**? (**Answers:** a male duck; a seagull; a poisonous plant.)

*There once was a very fat **snake**,*
*Who ate nothing but cookies and **cake**.*
Not a second went by
Without doughnut or pie,
*And he died of a big **tummyache**.*

–all rhymes (also –aul; –awl) _____

all	call	haul	shawl	tall
awl	crawl	mall	small	trawl
ball	drawl	maul	sprawl	wall
bawl	fall	recall	squall	
brawl	hall	scrawl		

Some harder words: appall, baseball, basketball, catcall, dancehall, downfall, enthrall, eyeball, install, nightfall, overall, overhaul, pall, pitfall, rainfall, waterfall, yawl

*Humpty Dumpty sat on a **wall**.*
*Humpty Dumpty had a great **fall**!*
—Nursery Rhyme

–ally rhymes (also –alley)

alley	rally	tally
dally	sally	valley
galley		

Quick quiz: Do you know what **sally** means? It's not the name Sally, but a useful word. Look it up if you don't know it! Actually, there are many first names which are also words. Can you think of some? (*Hint*: Think of different kinds of flowers.)

–am rhymes (also –ame; –amb)

am	gram	lam	ram	slam
clam	ham	lamb	scram	swam
cram	jam	madame	sham	
dam	jamb	pram		

Some harder words: cablegram, cam, diagram, diaphragm, dram, epigram, grandslam, kilogram, monogram, program, telegram

*Mary had a little **lamb**,*
*Little **lamb**, little **lamb**.*
*Mary had a little **lamb***
*Who grew into a **ram**.*

It could have been a ewe, you say,
Ewe you say, ewe you say?
It could have been a ewe, you say?
We'll know the truth one day.

*But what if it had been a **clam**,*
*Been a **clam**, been a **clam**?*
*But Mary never had a **clam**!*
*I'm sure it was a **lamb**!*

–ame rhymes (also –aim)

aim	claim	flame	lame	shame
blame	dame	frame	name	tame
came	fame	game	same	

Some harder words: acclaim, defame, exclaim, inflame, nickname, overcame, proclaim, reclaim, surname

–ammer rhymes (also –ammar; –amor; –amour)

clamor	grammar	slammer	yammer
enamor	hammer	stammer	
glamour	rammer		

–amp rhymes

camp	cramp	ramp	tamp
champ	damp	scamp	tramp
clamp	lamp	stamp	

He thought he saw an Albatross
That fluttered round the **lamp**:
He looked again, and found it was
A penny postage **stamp**.
"You'd best be getting home," he said,
"The nights are very **damp**.*"*

—Lewis Carroll
("Sylvie and Bruno")

–amper rhymes

camper	hamper	scamper
damper	pamper	tamper

–an rhymes

ban	clan	pecan	span	than
began	fan	plan	suntan	van
bran	man	ran	tan	
can	pan	scan		

Some harder words: afghan, caravan, cattleman, caveman, divan, dustpan, marzipan, middleman, rattan, sandman, sedan, superman, toucan

Be careful! There are any number of other words which *look* as if they rhyme but don't. Among them are **cardigan, human, organ, orphan, slogan.** The best way to tell for sure is to say them out loud. Do you hear the difference?

Mix a pancake,
Stir a pancake,
Pop it in the **pan***;*
Fry the pancake,
Toss the pancake,
Catch it if you **can***!*
—Christina Rossetti
("The Pancake")

—and rhymes

and	brand	expand	hand	stand
band	command	gland	land	strand
bland	demand	grand	sand	

Some harder words: eland, quicksand, reprimand, saraband, understand

Quick quiz: Do you know what an **eland** is? And how about a **saraband**? (The first is a kind of antelope, the second a stately dance.)

Isn't it **grand**
To sit on the **sand**,
And watch the clouds
Drift over the **land**?

–ander rhymes (also –andor)_____

candor	grander	sander
dander	meander	slander
gander	pander	

*"Please forgive my **candor**,"*
*Said the goose to the **gander**,*
"But you're not my cup of tea."
*"You'll find no **gander grander**,"*
*To the goose said the **gander**,*
"And I'll find another goose for me."

–ang rhymes (also –angue)

bang	gang	rang	sprang
clang	hang	sang	tang
fang	pang	slang	twang

Some harder words: boomerang, harangue, meringue, mustang, overhang, shebang

Quick quiz: Short words are often tricky. On this list, for instance, there are **pang** and **tang**. Do you know exactly what they mean? If not, why not look them up?

–angle rhymes

angle	mangle	strangle	wangle
bangle	spangle	tangle	wrangle
dangle			

–ank rhymes

bank	drank	plank	shrank	tank
blank	flank	prank	spank	thank
clank	frank	rank	stank	yank
crank	hank	sank	swank	
dank	lank	shank		

Some harder words: gangplank, pointblank, piggybank

–ant rhymes

ant	can't	pant	scant
aunt	chant	plant	slant
cant	grant		

Some harder words: enchant, eggplant, implant, supplant, transplant

–ap rhymes

cap	gap	rap	snap	trap
chap	lap	sap	strap	wrap
clap	map	scrap	tap	
flap	nap	slap		

Some harder words: burlap, handicap, kidnap, kneecap, mishap, mousetrap, nightcap, overlap, skullcap, thunderclap

*Stop all the **tapping**!*
*Stop all the **clapping**!*
Cannot you see
*That children are **napping**?*

−ape rhymes (also −epe)

ape	escape	nape	shape
cape	gape	scrape	tape
drape	grape		

Two harder words: crepe, landscape

−apper rhymes

clapper	flapper	scrapper	trapper
dapper	napper	snapper	wrapper

–ar rhymes

are	char	far	mar	spar
bar	cigar	guitar	par	star
car	czar	jar	scar	tar

Some harder words: bazaar, bizarre, boudoir, caviar, jaguar, memoir, registrar, samovar, sitar

> *Twang and twang goes my* **guitar**.
> *Clearly it's not up to* **par**.
> *If I plucked its brand new string,*
> *Would it play me songs to sing?*
> *Twang and twang goes my* **guitar**.
> *Sad to say, not up to* **par**.
>> (To be sung to the tune of
>> "Twinkle, Twinkle, Little Star")

–ard rhymes (also –uard)

bard	hard	shard
card	lard	yard
guard	regard	

Some harder words: backyard, bombard, boulevard, canard, chard, discard, disregard, foulard, lifeguard, mansard, placard, postcard, retard, shipyard, trump-card, vanguard

–ark rhymes

arc	dark	mark	snark
ark	hark	park	spark
bark	lark	shark	stark

Some harder words: birthmark, bookmark, embark, landmark, monarch, patriarch, pockmark, postmark, quark, remark

Quick quiz: What is a **snark**? Up until 1876, there was no such thing! Then Lewis Carroll, the famous author of *Alice in Wonderland*, invented it in a poem you'll love reading. It's called "The Hunting of the Snark." But—of course—there's no such thing as a snark.

When it rained and rained, he built the **ark**,
And all the animals had to **embark**,
Two by two, they marched up the plank,
Two by two, regardless of rank,
Tigers and lions, pigeons and **larks**,
And even, good gracious, two newly-wed **sharks**!

–arrow rhymes

arrow	harrow	narrow
barrow	marrow	sparrow

In Dublin's fair city, where girls are so pretty,
Twas there I laid eyes on Miss Molly Malone.
She wheeled a **wheelbarrow**
Through streets broad and **narrow**,
Crying "Cockles and mussels, alive alive-o."
—Anonymous
("Molly Malone")

–art rhymes (also –eart)

apart	chart	heart	smart
art	dart	mart	start
cart	hart	part	tart

Some harder words: counterpart, depart, oxcart, pushcart, rampart, sweetheart, upstart

> *The friendly cow, all red and white,*
> *I love with all my* **heart**.
> *She gives me cream with all her might*
> *To eat with apple* **tart**.
> —Robert Louis Stevenson
> ("The Cow")

–as rhymes (also –ass)

alas	brass	gas	lass
ass	class	glass	mass
bass	crass	grass	pass

Some harder words: harass, jackass, looking-glass, outclass, overpass, sassafras, surpass, trespass

–ash rhymes (also –ache)

abash	cash	gash	rash	splash
ash	clash	gnash	sash	thrash
bash	crash	hash	slash	trash
brash	dash	lash	smash	
cache	flash	mash		

Some harder words: balderdash, slapdash, succotash

Corns and beans are **succotash,**
Lots of nonsense: **balderdash.**
Raised red bumps are called a **rash.**
Stored-up treasure is a **cache.**

–ask rhymes (also –asque)_____

ask	casque	masque
bask	flask	task
cask	mask	

–ast rhymes_____

blast	last	past
cast	mast	vast
fast		

Some harder words: aghast, avast, bombast, broadcast, contrast, downcast, flabbergast, forecast, gymnast, outcast, outlast, overcast, repast, steadfast

Timely tip: If you're looking for more **–ast** words, check the **–as rhymes** for words to which you can add **–ed**, like **gassed** and **passed**.

–aste rhymes (also –aist)_____

baste	paste	waist
chaste	taste	waste
haste		

Some harder words: distaste, foretaste, lambaste, shirtwaist

Timely tip: If you're missing a rhyme, check out the **–ace** page for words to which you can add the letter **d**, like **faced** and **traced**.

–at rhymes

bat	fat	mat	slat
brat	flat	pat	spat
cat	gnat	rat	that
chat	hat	sat	vat

Some harder words: acrobat, combat, cravat, democrat, diplomat, habitat, muskrat, tophat, wildcat, wombat

*A **bat**,*
*Sitting on a **hat**,*
*Spied a **cat**,*
*A very **fat cat**,*
*Looking at a **rat**,*
*Who was watching a **gnat**,*
*Who **sat***
On the nose of a dog.

*The **bat** saw the **cat**.*
*The **cat** saw the **rat**.*
*The **rat** saw the **gnat**.*

*Can you beat **that**?*

Oh yes I can!
*The dog sneezed and scared the **gnat**,*
*Who flew from the **rat**,*
*Who fled from the **cat**,*
*Who was too **fat** to chase the **rat***
*Or do much at all but **chat** with the **bat**,*
*Sitting on the **hat**,*
Upside down,
And hanging from the brim.

–atter rhymes

batter	flatter	patter	shatter	splatter
chatter	hatter	platter	smatter	tatter
clatter	latter	scatter	spatter	
fatter	matter			

–ave rhymes (also –aive)

brave	gave	nave	shave	waive
cave	grave	rave	slave	wave
crave	knave	save		

Some harder words: behave, brainwave, concave, engrave, enslave, forgave, misbehave, shortwave, stave

Oh, say, does that star-spangled banner yet **wave**
O'er the land of the free and the home of the **brave**?
—Francis Scott Key
("The Star Spangled Banner")

–aw rhymes (also –awe)

awe	flaw	macaw	saw
caw	gnaw	maw	straw
claw	jaw	paw	thaw
draw	law	raw	

Some harder words: coleslaw, foresaw, guffaw, hacksaw, in-law, jigsaw, lockjaw, rickshaw, seesaw, taw, withdraw

–awn rhymes (also –one)

awn	drawn	lawn	sawn
brawn	fawn	pawn	spawn
dawn	gone	prawn	yawn

–ay rhymes (also –eigh; –ey)

bay	gray	obey	say	sway
clay	hay	pay	slay	they
day	jay	play	spay	way
dray	lay	pray	spray	weigh
fray	may	prey	stay	whey
gay	neigh	ray	stray	

Some harder words: allay, anyway, array, assay, astray, betray, bluejay, decay, delay, dismay, display, doorway, essay, foray, gangway, highway, holiday, inlay, leeway, mainstay, mislay, outlay, pathway, portray, railway, relay, runaway, subway, today, yesterday

Great is the palace with pillar and wall,
A sort of tower on top of it,
And steps coming down in an orderly **way**
To where my toy vessels lie safe in the **bay**.
　　　　　　　　—Robert Louis Stevenson
　　　　　　　　　　("Block City")

–aze rhymes (also –aise; –aize) _____

amaze	craze	gaze	maize	raise
blaze	daze	glaze	maze	raze
braise	faze	haze	praise	

Timely tip: You can make more rhymes simply by adding an **s** onto any number of words ending in **–ay**.

–e rhymes (also –ea; –ee; –ey) _____

agree	free	lee	see	we
be	glee	me	she	wee
bee	he	pea	spree	
fee	key	plea	tree	
flea	knee	sea		

Some harder words: acme, banshee, bumblebee, carefree, chimpanzee, dungaree, fricassee, goatee, guarantee, jubilee, oversee, referee, sesame, tepee

> *O, Susanna! O, don't you cry for **me**,*
> *For I've come from Alabama,*
> *with my banjo on my **knee**.*
>
> —Stephen Foster
> ("O, Susanna")

–each rhymes (also –eech) _____

beach	breech	peach	screech
beech	each	preach	speech
bleach	leech	reach	teach

Two harder words: beseech, impeach

"O Oysters, come and walk with us!"
The Walrus did **beseech.**
"A pleasant walk, a pleasant talk,
Along the briny **beach."**
—Lewis Carroll
("The Walrus and the Carpenter")

–ead rhymes (also –ede; –eed)

bead	deed	kneed	read	steed
bleed	feed	lead	reed	treed
breed	greed	mead	seed	weed
cede	heed	need	speed	
creed	indeed	plead		

Some harder words: agreed, concede, decreed, exceed, hayseed, impede, precede, proceed, seaweed, secede, stampede, succeed, supersede

–eak rhymes (also –eek; –ic; –iek; –ique)

beak	creek	peak	sleek	teak
bleak	freak	peek	sneak	tweek
cheek	leak	reek	speak	weak
chic	leek	seek	squeak	week
creak	meek	shriek	streak	

Some harder words: antique, clique, critique, oblique, physique, pique, technique, unique, wreak

–eal rhymes (also –eel; –ile) _____

deal	heel	peal	seal	teal
eel	keel	peel	squeal	veal
feel	kneel	real	steal	wheel
heal	meal	reel	steel	zeal

Some harder words: appeal, automobile, cartwheel, conceal, congeal, creel, genteel, newsreel, oatmeal, piecemeal, repeal, reveal, weal

"I wish I could drive,"
*Said the **eel***
*To the **seal**.*
"We'd go for a ride
*In my **automobile**."*

—eam rhymes (also —eem; —ime)

beam	dream	scream	steam	team
cream	gleam	seam	stream	teem
deem	ream	seem		

Some harder words: coldcream, crossbeam, esteem, moonbeam, redeem, regime

I **scream**,
You **scream**,
We all **scream**
For ice **cream***!*
—Anonymous

–ean rhymes (also –een; –ene; –ien; –ine)

bean	green	mean	screen	teen
clean	jean	preen	sheen	wean
dean	keen	seen	spleen	
glean	lean	scene		

Some harder words: between, canteen, careen, chlorine, convene, cuisine, gangrene, hygiene, intervene, kerosene, lien, machine, marine, mien, pristine, ravine, routine, serene, submarine, tangerine, tureen, vaccine

Jack Sprat could eat no fat,
*His wife could eat no **lean**.*
And so betwixt the two of them,
*They licked the platter **clean**.*
                                        —Nursery Rhyme

–eap rhymes (also –eep)

asleep	creep	keep	seep	sweep
beep	deep	leap	sheep	weep
bleep	heap	peep	sleep	
cheap	jeep	reap	steep	

*When at night the shadows **creep**,*
*And gray shapes o'er my pillow **leap**,*
Then I in bed
Am filled with dread
By hooves that thunder through my head,
*Until at last I fall **asleep**.*
*But how? But why? By counting **sheep**.*

–eaper rhymes (also –eeper)

beeper	deeper	peeper	steeper
cheaper	keeper	reaper	sweeper
creeper	leaper	sleeper	weeper

–ear rhymes (also –eer; –ere; –ier)

beer	fear	mere	sheer	tear
cheer	gear	near	smear	tier
clear	hear	peer	sneer	veer
dear	here	pier	spear	year
deer	jeer	sear	sphere	
ear	leer	shear	steer	

Some harder words: adhere, appear, bier, career, cashier, disappear, engineer, financier, musketeer, overseer, reindeer, revere, sere, severe, sincere, volunteer

–ease rhymes (also –eace; –eece; –eese; –ese; –iece)

cease	fleece	grease	niece	piece
crease	geese	lease	peace	

Some harder words: decease, decrease, increase, mantelpiece, masterpiece, mouthpiece, obese, release

–eat rhymes (also –eet; –eipt; –eit; –ete; –uite)

beat	feat	meet	sheet	sweet
beet	feet	mete	skeet	treat
bleat	fleet	neat	sleet	tweet
cheat	greet	peat	street	wheat
cleat	heat	seat	suite	
eat	meat			

Some harder words: athlete, compete, complete, deceit, defeat, delete, deplete, discreet, mistreat, obsolete, parakeet, receipt, repeat, secrete

*Chill December brings the **sleet**,*
*Blazing fire, and Christmas **Treat**.*
> —Sara Coleridge
> ("The Months")

–eater rhymes (also –eeter; –eter; –iter)

beater	fleeter	liter	repeater	teeter
cheater	greeter	meter	seater	tweeter
eater	heater	neater	sweeter	

–eather rhymes (also –ether)

feather	leather	tether	weather
heather	nether	together	whether

–eave rhymes (also –eeve; –eive; –eve; –ieve)

eave	heave	sleeve
eve	leave	weave
grieve	peeve	

Some harder words: achieve, believe, bereave, cleave, conceive, deceive, perceive, receive, relieve, reprieve, retrieve

–eck rhymes (also –eque)

beck	fleck	speck
check	neck	trek
deck	peck	wreck

Some harder words: bedeck, discotheque, gooseneck, henpeck, roughneck, shipwreck

> *A tailor, who sailed from **Quebec**,*
> *In a storm ventured once upon **deck**,*
> *But the waves of the sea*
> *Were as strong as can be,*
> *And he tumbled in up to his **neck**.*
> —R. S. Sharpe

–ed rhymes (also –aid; –ead)_____

bed	dread	led	sled	tread
bled	fed	read	spread	wed
bread	fled	red	sped	
bred	head	said	stead	
dead	lead	shed	thread	

Some harder words: bedspread, behead, biped, bloodshed, bobsled, bulkhead, figurehead, forehead, gingerbread, instead, masthead, thoroughbred, towhead, unwed

I have a little shadow that goes in and out with
    me,
And what can be the use of him is more than I
    can see.
He is very, very like me from the heels up to the
    head,
And I see him jump before me when I jump into
    *my **bed**.*

—Robert Louis Stevenson
("My Shadow")

–edge rhymes

dredge	ledge	wedge
edge	pledge	
hedge	sledge	

–eeze rhymes (also –ease; –eese; –ese; –eize; –ieze; –ise)

breeze	freeze	sneeze	these
cheese	please	squeeze	wheeze
ease	seize	tease	

Some harder words: appease, cerise, chemise, disease, expertise, frieze, trapeze, valise

Timely tip: Of course you can add enormously to the **–eeze rhymes** list by using the plural of many of the **–e rhyme** words. Like: the **bee's knees.**

*He flies through the air with the greatest of **ease**,*
*This daring young man on the flying **trapeze**.*
*His figure is handsome, all girls he can **please**,*
And my love he purloined her away!

—George Leybourne
("The Man on the Flying Trapeze")

–eg rhymes (also –egg)

beg	keg	peg
dreg	leg	yegg
egg	nutmeg	

–ell rhymes (also –el; –elle)_____

bell	ell	knell	smell	well
cell	fell	quell	spell	yell
dell	hell	sell	swell	
dwell	jell	shell	tell	

Some harder words: befell, citadel, compel, dispel, excel, expel, foretell, lapel, mademoiselle, nutshell, pastel, personnel, propel, rebel, repel, retell, seashell

*Who ran to help me when I **fell**?*
*And would some pretty story **tell**,*
*Or kiss the place to make it **well**?*
My mother.

—Ann Taylor
("My Mother")

–elt rhymes (also –ealt; –eldt; –elte)_____

belt	felt	pelt	svelte
dealt	knelt	smelt	veldt
dwelt	melt	spelt	welt

Quick quiz: There are two strange-looking words on this list—**svelte** and **veldt**. **Svelte** is originally a French word; **veldt** is Dutch. Do you know what they mean? If not, why not look them up?

> *On the **veldt***
> *There **dwelt***
> *A **svelte***
> *Gazelle.*

–em rhymes (also –egm)_____

ahem	stem
gem	them
hem	

Some harder words: condemn, diadem, phlegm, requiem, stratagem

–en rhymes

amen	glen	pen	wen	yen
den	hen	ten	when	
fen	men	then	wren	

Be careful! There's a problem with the longer **–en** words. They're almost never pronounced like "**en**!" For example, would you say **women** rhymes with **men**? Say them out loud. Do you see the difference? Almost every compound word ending in **–en** is pronounced either like "**in**" or like "**n**," as though there was no vowel at all.

–ench rhymes

bench	quench	wench
clench	stench	wrench
drench	trench	

–end rhymes

bend	fend	mend	spend	vend
blend	friend	rend	tend	wend
end	lend	send	trend	

Some harder words: amend, append, ascend, attend, befriend, commend, comprehend, condescend, contend, defend, depend, descend, dividend, expend, extend, intend, offend, pretend, recommend, suspend, transcend

–ender rhymes (also –endor)

bender	gender	sender	tender
blender	lender	slender	vendor
fender	mender	spender	

Some harder words: pretender, surrender

–ent rhymes

bent	gent	pent	sent	vent
cent	lent	rent	spent	went
dent	meant	scent	tent	

Some harder words: accent, ascent, circumvent, consent, content, dissent, extent, foment, intent, invent, percent, prevent, relent, repent, resent, torment

Be careful! A lot of words ending in **–ent** look good, but when you say them out loud, they don't really rhyme. Watch out for words like **intelligent**, **parent**, **urgent**. Use them at your own risk!

–erge rhymes (also –irge; –urge)

dirge	serge	verge
merge	surge	urge
scourge	splurge	

Some harder words: converge, diverge, emerge, submerge

–erry rhymes (also –ery; –ury)

berry	ferry	terry
bury	merry	very
cherry	sherry	

Some harder words: adversary, arbitrary, blackberry, blueberry, contemporary, customary, dignitary, dromedary, emissary, fragmentary, itinerary, library, literary, mercenary, military, momentary, mulberry, primary, raspberry, sanitary, secretary, solitary, strawberry, tributary

How many fruits can you rhyme with **berry***?*
*Black****berry****, blue****berry****, cran****berry****, **cherry***.*
*But what about straw****berry****, rasp****berry****, goose****berry****?*
*What about huckle****berry****?*
Everybody's *got a* **berry***!*
How many fruits can you rhyme with **berry***?*
*Black****berry****, blue****berry****, cran****berry****, **cherry***.*

–erse rhymes (also –earse; –erce; –orse; –urse)

curse	purse	worse
hearse	terse	
nurse	verse	

Some harder words: adverse, coerce, converse, disperse, diverse, inverse, perverse, rehearse, reimburse, reverse, traverse, universe

–ert rhymes (also –irt; –uirt; –urt)_____

alert	dessert	flirt	pert	spurt
blurt	exert	girt	shirt	squirt
curt	dirt	hurt	skirt	

Some harder words: assert, avert, concert, convert, disconcert, divert, expert, inert, insert, invert, outskirt, revert, undershirt

–erve rhymes (also –urve)

curve	swerve
nerve	verve
serve	

Some harder words: conserve, deserve, observe, preserve, reserve, unnerve

–ess rhymes (also –es; –esce)

bless	guess	stress
chess	mess	tress
dress	press	yes

Some harder words: access, acquiesce, address, convalesce, digress, distress, duress, effervesce, excess, express, finesse, impress, largesse, obsess, oppress, profess, progress, repress, success, unless

Timely tip: You can add a zillion other words ending in –ness and –less to this list!

–est rhymes (also –east)

best	guest	quest	vest
breast	jest	pest	west
chest	lest	rest	wrest
crest	nest	test	zest

Some harder words: arrest, attest, detest, digest, infest, invest, protest, suggest, unrest

Timely tip: There are lots of words ending in **–ess** to which you only have to add an **–ed** for them to fit here. For example: **blessed, dressed, guessed.**

> *The sun descending in the **west**,*
> *The evening star does shine;*
> *The birds are silent in their **nest**,*
> *And I must seek for mine.*
> —William Blake
> ("Night")

–et rhymes (also –eat; –ette)

abet	fret	met	sweat	whet
bet	get	net	threat	yet
debt	jet	pet	vet	
duet	let	set	wet	

Some harder words: alphabet, amulet, asset, beget, cadet, cigarette, cornet, forget, inlet, inset, outlet, quartet, regret, reset, roulette, sextet, vignette

–etch rhymes

etch	sketch
fetch	stretch
ketch	wretch

–etter rhymes (also –eater; –ettor)

better	fretter	setter
bettor	getter	sweater
fetter	letter	wetter

–ettle rhymes (also –etal)

fettle	mettle	settle
kettle	nettle	
metal	petal	

> *"You're testing my **mettle**,"*
> *Said the pot to the **kettle**,*
> *"When you whistle a tune at my back.*
> *I'm in very fine **fettle**,*
> *I'm shiny new **metal**,*
> *I'm thinking of calling you black!"*

–ew rhymes (also –o; –oo; –ou; –ough; –u; –ue)

ado	few	moo	slue	two
blew	flew	new	spew	view
blue	flu	pew	stew	who
brew	flue	rue	strew	woo
clue	glue	screw	sue	yew
crew	gnu	shoe	threw	you
dew	hew	shoo	through	zoo
do	hue	shrew	to	
drew	knew	skew	too	
due	mew	slew	true	

Some harder words: ague, argue, askew, avenue, barbecue, bayou, continue, curfew, ensue, issue, kazoo, mildew, nephew, pursue, queue, renew, rescue, revenue, review, sinew, statue, subdue, tissue, value, virtue

Something old,
*Something **new,***
Something borrowed,
*Something **blue,***
And a lucky sixpence
*In her **shoe.***

—Anonymous

–ib rhymes

adlib	fib	rib
bib	glib	squib
crib	jib	

*Babies wear **bibs***
*And sleep in their **cribs***
And giggle and bleat
When you tickle their feet.

–ice rhymes (also –ise)

dice	nice	slice	thrice	vice
ice	price	spice	trice	
mice	rice	splice	twice	

Some harder words: advice, concise, device, entice, paradise, precise, sacrifice, suffice

*Sugar and **spice***
*And everything **nice**,*
That's what little girls are made of.
—Nursery Rhyme

–ick rhymes (also –ic)

chick	kick	prick	stick	wick
click	lick	quick	tic	
crick	nick	sick	tick	
flick	pick	slick	trick	

Some harder words: aspic, attic, basic, caustic, civic, classic, cosmic, cubic, cynic, domestic, epic, epidemic, fabric, garlic, hectic, heroic, lyric, magic, metric, mimic, mystic, optic, picnic, relic, republic, rustic, stoic, toxic, tunic. (In fact, there are many more words ending in **–ic** than we can possibly list. Find your own!)

Jack be nimble,
*Jack be **quick**,*
Jack jump over
*The **candlestick**.*
　　　　—Nursery Rhyme

–icker rhymes (also –iquor)

bicker	kicker	picker	slicker	thicker
dicker	licker	quicker	snicker	ticker
flicker	liquor	sicker	sticker	wicker

–id rhymes

acid	did	lid	slid
amid	hid	rid	solid
bid	kid	skid	squid

Some harder words: acrid, aphid, avid, candid, florid, forbid, hybrid, limpid, lucid, lurid, morbid, orchid, placid, putrid, pyramid, rabid, rancid, rapid

–ide rhymes (also –eyed; –ied; –ighed; –yed)

aside	dyed	hide	ride	tied
bride	eyed	lied	side	tried
chide	fried	plied	sighed	vied
cried	glide	pride	slide	wide
died	guide	pried	tide	

Some harder words: abide, allied, applied, beside, coincide, collide, confide, countryside, decide, divide, fireside, homicide, inside, landslide, outside, oxide, peroxide, preside, provide, reside, subside, suicide

*Land where my fathers **died**,*
*Land of the pilgrims' **pride**,*
*From every **mountainside**,*
Let freedom ring.
—Samuel Francis Smith
("America the Beautiful")

–ider rhymes

cider	rider	strider
eider	slider	wider
glider	spider	

Quick quiz: Do you know what an eider is? It's a kind of duck. But the best thing about the eider is eiderdown—that is, duck feathers—which, when stuffed into a quilt, will keep you warm on the coldest winter nights.

> *Along came a **spider***
> *Who sat down **beside her***
> *And frightened Miss Muffet away.*
> —Nursery Rhyme

–ife rhymes

fife	rife
knife	strife
life	wife

Some harder words: housewife, jackknife, midwife, wildlife

> *Who was that ladle I saw you with?*
> *That was no ladle,*
> *That was my **knife**!*
>
> *Who was that fiddle I saw you with?*
> *That was no fiddle,*
> *That was my **fife**!*
>
> —Anonymous

–iff rhymes (also –if; –yph)

cliff	skiff	tiff
if	sniff	whiff
miff	stiff	

Some harder words: bailiff, hieroglyph, mastiff, midriff, plaintiff, sheriff, tariff

–ift rhymes (also –iffed)

drift	miffed	sift	thrift
gift	rift	sniffed	
lift	shift	swift	

Some harder words: adrift, makeshift, shoplift, snowdrift, spendthrift, uplift

–ig rhymes

big	gig	prig	swig
dig	jig	rig	twig
fig	pig	sprig	wig

On seeing the sun,
*The cow did a **jig**,*
Urged on by the rooster,
*Who woke up the **pig**,*
Who snorted and rooted
*And took a long **swig***
Of the milk that was meant for the cat!

–ight rhymes (also –ite; –uite)

bite	fright	mite	sight	trite
blight	height	night	site	white
bright	kite	plight	smite	write
byte	knight	quite	spite	
fight	light	right	sprite	
flight	might	rite	tight	

Some harder words: appetite, contrite, delight, despite, dynamite, excite, finite, flashlight, frostbite, graphite, incite, invite, midnight, parasite, polite, recite, satellite, termite, tonight, twilight

> *Tiger, Tiger, burning **bright***
> *In the forests of the **night**.*
> —William Blake
> ("The Tiger")

–ike rhymes

alike	hike	spike
bike	like	strike
dike	pike	tyke

Some harder words: childlike, dislike, hitchhike, turnpike, unlike

–ile rhymes (also –isle; –yle)

aisle	isle	rile	tile
file	mile	smile	vile
guile	pile	style	while

Some harder words: argyle, awhile, beguile, compile, crocodile, defile, exile, juvenile, lisle, meanwhile, profile, reconcile, reptile, senile, stile, turnstile, wile

*When I saw them reach the **aisle**,*
*I thought I saw their secret **smile**.*
Their hands touched one another.
*And he stood tall, a man of **style**,*
My father with my mother.

–ill rhymes (also –il)

bill	gill	nil	spill	twill
chill	grill	pill	still	will
dill	hill	rill	swill	
drill	ill	shrill	thrill	
fill	kill	sill	till	
frill	mill	skill	trill	

Some harder words: daffodil, foothill, fulfill, instill, treadmill, until, whippoorwill, windowsill

> *Out goes the river*
> *And out past the **mill**,*
> *Away down the valley*
> *Away down the **hill**.*
> —Robert Louis Stevenson
> ("Where Go the Boats?")

–ilt rhymes (also –uilt)

built	hilt	lilt	spilt
gilt	jilt	quilt	stilt
guilt	kilt	silt	tilt

> *How many pieces*
> *make up a **quilt**?*
> *How many pleats*
> *can you find in a **kilt**?*
> *How many bricks*
> *in the house that Jack **built**?*
> *Questions galore,*
> *Oh please, please,*
> *no more!*

–im rhymes (also –imn; –ymn)

brim	him	rim	swim
dim	hymn	skim	trim
grim	prim	slim	whim

Some harder words: interim, limn, maxim, pilgrim, pseudonym, synonym, victim

–ime rhymes (also –yme)

chime	grime	prime	slime
crime	lime	rhyme	thyme
dime	mime	rime	time

Some harder words: bedtime, lifetime, meantime, pantomime, pastime, ragtime, sometime, sublime

When you act without words,
*That's **mime**.*
When words sound the same,
*That's **rhyme**!*

–in rhymes (also –ine; –inn)

begin	fin	inn	sin	tin
bin	gin	kin	skin	twin
chin	grin	pin	spin	win
din	in	shin	thin	

Some harder words: basin, buckskin, bulletin, cabin, chagrin, coffin, cousin, gelatin, gherkin, goblin, jasmine, margin, maudlin, mocassin, muffin, napkin, origin, paraffin, poplin, pumpkin, raisin, resin, tailspin, urchin, vermin, virgin, within

How many hairs on a monkey's **chin**?
How many travelers stop at the **inn**?
How many worlds on the head of a **pin**?
If you'll tell me,
I'll say, "You **win**!"

–ince rhymes (also –inse; –intz)_____

chintz	quince	wince
mince	rinse	
prince	since	

Some harder words: convince, evince, province

Timely tip: There's not a lot to choose from here, but you can double the list by adding an **s** to many words ending in **–int**. Like **mints** and **squints**.

–inch rhymes (also –ynch)_____

cinch	flinch	pinch
clinch	inch	winch
finch	lynch	

–ind rhymes_____

bind	grind	mind
blind	hind	rind
find	kind	wind

Timely tip: By adding an **–ed** to many words ending in **–ign**, or a **–d** to words ending in **–ine**, you can get many more rhymes. Try **signed** or **mined**, for instance.

–ine rhymes (also –ein; –ign)

dine	nine	sign	thine	whine
fine	pine	sine	tine	wine
line	shine	spine	twine	
mine	shrine	swine	vine	

Some harder words: airline, align, assign, benign, canine, combine, confine, decline, define, design, divine, feline, headline, incline, iodine, kine, outline, porcupine, recline, refine, resign, stein, turbine, valentine

> *Drink to me only with **thine** eyes*
> *And I will pledge with **mine**;*
> *Or leave a kiss but in the cup*
> *And I'll not look for **wine**.*
> —Ben Jonson
> ("To Celia")

–ing rhymes

bring	king	sing	sting	thing
cling	ping	sling	string	wing
fling	ring	spring	swing	

Timely tip: This is probably the biggest rhyme sound in the English language. Can you think why? Well, all you have to do is add an **–ing** to any verb and there you are. Try **going**, **flowing**, **painting** for starters.

"The time has come," the Walrus said,
"To talk of many **things***:*
Of shoes—and ships—and sealing wax—
Of cabbages—and **kings***—*
And why the sea is boiling hot—
And whether pigs have **wings***.*

—Lewis Carroll
("The Walrus and the Carpenter")

–inge rhymes

binge	hinge	twinge
cringe	singe	
fringe	tinge	

Some harder words: infringe, syringe, unhinge

–inger rhymes

finger	singer	swinger
linger	slinger	wringer
ringer	stinger	

–ink rhymes (also –inc)

blink	drink	mink	sink	wink
brink	ink	pink	slink	zinc
chink	kink	rink	stink	
clink	link	shrink	think	

If all the world were paper,
*And all the sea were **ink**,*
If all the trees were bread and cheese,
*What would we have to **drink**?*

—Anonymous (17th Century)

–inner rhymes

dinner	spinner
inner	thinner
sinner	winner

–int rhymes

dint	hint	print	squint
flint	lint	splint	stint
glint	mint	sprint	tint

Some harder words: blueprint, fingerprint, footprint, imprint, peppermint, reprint, skinflint, reprint, varmint

–ip rhymes

chip	flip	nip	sip	strip
clip	grip	quip	skip	trip
dip	hip	rip	slip	whip
drip	lip	ship	snip	zip

Some harder words: catnip, censorship, courtship, equip, hardship, kinship, parsnip, partnership, penmanship, scholarship, scrip, tulip, warship, worship

–ipe rhymes (also –ype)

gripe	ripe	swipe	wipe
hype	snipe	tripe	
pipe	stripe	type	

Some harder words: bagpipe, hornpipe, overripe, sideswipe, stereotype, unripe

–iper rhymes (also –iaper)

diaper	riper	viper
griper	sniper	wiper
piper	striper	

–ipper rhymes

clipper	kipper	shipper	stripper
dipper	nipper	skipper	tripper
flipper	ripper	slipper	zipper

–ird rhymes (also –eard; –erd; –ord; –urd)

bird	heard	word
curd	herd	
gird	third	

Some harder words: absurd, blackbird, crossword, foreword, jailbird, overheard, password, railbird, surd

Timely tip: In addition to these, there are words in the **–ir** and **–ur** family to which you can add **–ed** or **–red** to make more rhymes, like **purred** and **shirred**.

*Did I tell you the tale of the **bird**,*
*Who wished to belong to the **herd***
Of elephants, tigers, and rhinoceri,
Of zebras and pandas and pigs that can fly?
*Now isn't this story **absurd**?*

–ire rhymes (also –iar; –ier; –ior; –oir; –yer; –yre)

briar	flier	ire	prior	spier
choir	friar	liar	pyre	spire
crier	frier	lyre	shire	squire
dire	higher	mire	shyer	tire
fire	hire	plier	sire	wire

Some harder words: acquire, admire, aspire, attire, byre, desire, empire, expire, gyre, haywire, inspire, perspire, require, retire, sapphire, satire, umpire, vampire

I'd like to play an instrument,
Perhaps a flute or **lyre.**
I'd like to sing a pretty song,
Accompanied by a **choir.**
It's fun to think of all the things
To which I can **aspire,**
And though I'll never do them all,
They fill my heart's **desire.**

–irst rhymes (also –orst; –ursed; –urst)___

burst   nursed   worst
cursed   pursed
first   thirst

Some harder words: liverwurst, outburst

–is rhymes (also –ice; –ise; –iss)_____

axis   kiss   this
hiss   miss
iris   tennis

Some harder words: abyss, analysis, apprentice, avarice, chalice, cornice, cowardice, crevice, crisis, dais, hypnosis, ibis, justice, licorice, malice, mantis, notice, office, practice, precipice, prejudice, premise, promise, pumice, service, terrace, thesis, trellis

–ise rhymes (also –ize)

arise	rise	wise
guise	size	
prize	vise	

Some harder words: advertise, advise, apologize, authorize, capsize, chastize, comprise, criticize, despise, devise, emphasize, enterprise, exercise, franchise, idolize, improvise, likewise, merchandise, organize, recognize, revise, sunrise, supervise, surmise, surprise, utilize

Timely tip: Of course, there are many, many more rhymes to be made out of the plurals of words ending in **–uy** or **–y**. Think of **buys**, **flies**, **skies**…and off you go!

> *"I weep for you," the Walrus said:*
> *"I deeply **sympathize**."*
> *With sobs and tears he sorted out*
> *Those of the largest **size**,*
> *Holding his pocket handkerchief*
> *Before his streaming **eyes**.*
>   —Lewis Carroll
>   ("The Walrus and the Carpenter")

–ish rhymes

dish   wish
fish
swish

Some harder words: accomplish, admonish, astonish, banish, blemish, burnish, embellish, establish, famish, finish, flourish, foolish, furnish, garish, garnish, lavish, parish, publish, punish, radish, relish, selfish, tarnish, varnish

–ist rhymes (also –yst)

cyst	grist	list	twist
fist	hissed	mist	whist
gist	kissed	tryst	wrist

Some harder words: consist, desist, enlist, exist, insist, persist, resist, subsist

–it rhymes

bit	grit	nit	slit	wit
chit	hit	pit	spit	writ
exit	kit	quit	split	
fit	knit	sit	unit	
flit	lit	skit	whit	

Some harder words: admit, audit, bandit, benefit, biscuit, commit, credit, culprit, debit, decrepit, deposit, digit, edit, emit, explicit, forfeit, habit, hermit, inhabit, limit, misfit, omit, outfit, permit, prohibit, pulpit, rabbit, remit, spirit, submit, summit, tidbit, transit, visit, vomit

–itch rhymes (also –ich; –iche)

ditch	itch	rich	twitch
glitch	niche	stitch	which
hitch	pitch	switch	witch

A creature in black,
A creature in red,
One of them carries
A broomstick to bed.
One drinks a potion,
One mixes lotion,
One wears a cone,
One sits on a throne,
But the question to answer
Whenever they **switch,**
Is how can you tell then
Which witch *is* **which?**

–itter rhymes

bitter	flitter	hitter	sitter	titter
critter	fritter	litter	spitter	twitter
fitter	glitter	quitter	splitter	

–itty rhymes (also –etty; –ity)

city	kitty	witty
ditty	pity	
gritty	pretty	

–ive rhymes

alive	five	live
chive	hive	strive
dive	jive	thrive

Some harder words: archive, arrive, beehive, contrive, deprive, revive, survive

Timely tip: If you're looking for plural rhymes— that is, rhymes for **dives** and **strives**, for example, then check out the plurals of **–ife rhymes**. Words like **knives** and **wives** will work for you.

–iver rhymes

deliver	liver	shiver
flivver	quiver	sliver
giver	river	

–o rhymes (also –eau; –oe; –ough; –ow)

ago	crow	hello	owe	sorrow
although	doe	hero	pillow	sow
banjo	dough	hobo	pro	though
beau	echo	hoe	roe	throw
below	elbow	hollow	row	tomato
blow	flow	know	sew	tomorrow
borrow	foe	lasso	shadow	tow
bow	fro	low	show	widow
burro	glow	meadow	slow	willow
burrow	go	mow	snow	window
calico	grow	no	so	woe

Timely tip: There are many more –o rhymes, some no harder than these, but enough is enough! Why not start your own list of all we've left out?

> I stood beside a hill
> Smooth with new-laid **snow**
> A single star looked out
> From the cold evening **glow**.
> —Sara Teasdale
> ("February Twilight")

–oard rhymes (also –ard; –ord; –orde)

board	fjord	hoard	sword
chord	ford	horde	toward
cord	gourd	lord	

Some harder words: aboard, accord, afford, award, billboard, blackboard, cardboard, discord, harpsichord, overboard, record

Timely tip: A much longer list could be made if you added **–d** or **–ed** to many words ending in **–oor**; **–ore**; **–our**, such as **floored**, **bored**, **poured**.

–oast rhymes (also –ost)

boast	host	roast
coast	most	toast
ghost	post	

Some harder words: almost, foremost, outpost, potroast, utmost

> *I once knew a **ghost**,*
> *Who liked tea and **toast**,*
> *But what he liked more*
> *Was to float through the door.*

–oat rhymes (also –ote)

boat	gloat	note	shoat	vote
coat	goat	oat	stoat	wrote
dote	moat	quote	throat	
float	mote	rote	tote	

Some harder words: afloat, anecdote, antidote, denote, devote, ferryboat, footnote, motorboat, overcoat, petticoat, promote, remote, rowboat, sailboat, scapegoat, turncoat

–ob rhymes (also –ab)

blob	gob	lob	snob	throb
bob	hob	mob	sob	
cob	job	rob	squab	
fob	knob	slob	swab	

—ock rhymes (also —oc)

block	dock	knock	rock	stock
clock	flock	lock	shock	
cock	frock	mock	smock	
crock	hock	pock	sock	

Some harder words: bedrock, bock, deadlock, fetlock, hemlock, livestock, padlock, peacock, roc, unlock, wedlock

*What are you able to build with your **blocks**?*
*Castles and palaces, temples and **docks**.*
Rain may keep raining and others go roam,
But I can be happy and building at home.
　　　　　　　　　　—Robert Louis Stevenson
　　　　　　　　　　　　　("Block City")

–od rhymes (also –ad)

clod	nod	pod	shod	trod
cod	odd	prod	sod	wad
god	plod	rod	squad	

Some harder words: demigod, goldenrod, hod, quad, roughshod, slipshod

–ode rhymes (also –oad; –oed; –owed)

bode	goad	mode	rowed	sowed
code	hoed	node	showed	strode
crowed	load	ode	slowed	toad
flowed	lode	road	snowed	toed

Some harder words: abode, corrode, elbowed, episode, erode, explode, lowed, railroad

–og rhymes (also –ogue)

bog	flog	hog
clog	fog	jog
cog	frog	log

Some harder words: agog, backlog, bullfrog, catalogue, dialogue, eggnog, epilogue, hedgehog, leapfrog, monologue, prologue, synagogue

Hi, ho,
Frogs *in the* **bog**.
Hi, ho,
Hogs *on a* **log**.
Frogs *and* **hogs**,
Hogs *and* **frogs**,
And what do you know?
They're wearing **clogs**!

–oil rhymes (also –oyle)

boil	foil	soil
broil	oil	spoil
coil	roil	toil

Some harder words: embroil, gargoyle, hardboil, recoil, turmoil, uncoil

Foil it.
Oil it.
Boil it.
Broil it.

But whatever you do,
*Don't **spoil** it!*

–oke rhymes (also –oak; –olk; –oque)

bloke	croak	poke	stoke	yolk
broke	folk	smoke	stroke	
cloak	joke	soak	woke	
coke	oak	spoke	yoke	

Some harder words: artichoke, awoke, baroque, convoke, evoke, provoke, revoke, sunstroke

–old rhymes

bold	gold	old	told	fold
cold	hold	scold	mold	sold

Some harder words: behold, foothold, foretold, household, marigold, scaffold, stranglehold, threshold, unfold, untold, withhold

Timely tip: Make more rhyming words by adding **–d** or **–ed** to words ending in **–oal** or **–ole**, such as **foaled** and **poled**.

There once was a novel, I'm **told,**
Called The Spy Who Came in from the **Cold,**
About one George Smiley,
A chap very wily,
By George, but that Smiley was **bold!**

–older rhymes (also –oulder)

bolder	colder	holder	older	smolder
boulder	folder	molder	shoulder	

–ole rhymes (also –oal; –oll; –oul)

bowl	hole	role	soul	whole
coal	knoll	roll	stole	
dole	mole	scroll	stroll	
foal	pole	shoal	toll	
goal	poll	sole	troll	

Some harder words: cajole, casserole, charcoal, console, droll, enroll, keyhole, manhole, tadpole

> *Old King **Cole***
> *Wasn't merry at all*
> *When he called for his fiddlers three.*
> *His pipe had a **hole***
> *And they couldn't find his **bowl***
> *And his fiddlers played off key.*

–ome rhymes (also –oam; –omb)

chrome	dome	gnome	loam	tome
comb	foam	home	roam	

> *Oh give me a **home***
> *Where the buffalo **roam***
> *And the deer and the antelope play.*
> —Anonymous
> ("Home on the Range")

–on rhymes (also –an)

con	ion	wan
don	on	yon
eon	swan	

Some harder words: anon, capon, carillon, coupon, electron, icon, marathon, neuron, nylon, python, rayon, zircon

Be careful! There are many words ending in **–on** which look like rhymers but which aren't. Words like **bacon, beckon, reason, season.** The only way to be sure is to say them out loud.

> *On* and *on*
> *Swam the* **swan,**
> *An endless summer's* **marathon.**
> *The day grew old,*
> *The sun went cold,*
> *But* **on** *and* **on,**
> *On* and *on*.

–ond rhymes (also –and; –onde)

beyond	frond
blonde	pond
bond	wand

Some harder words: correspond, respond, vagabond

–one rhymes (also –oan; –own)

blown	groan	moan	roan	thrown
bone	grown	mown	scone	tone
cone	hone	own	shone	zone
crone	known	phone	shown	
drone	loan	pone	stone	
flown	lone	prone	throne	

Some harder words: alone, atone, backbone, baritone, brownstone, condone, cyclone, funnybone, limestone, megaphone, microphone, overtone, postpone, saxophone, tombstone, xylophone

–ong rhymes

along	song
belong	strong
long	wrong

Be careful! The **–ong** rhymes are in two groups which look exactly alike but sound different. Say a word out loud to be sure which group it belongs to. A list of the second group (**–ong** as in **gong**) follows.

Oh, bang the drum slowly
And play the fife lowly,
*Play the Dead March as you carry me **along**.*
Take me to the green valley,
There lay the sod over me,
For I'm a young cowboy and I know I've done
   ***wrong**.*

—Anonymous
("The Cowboy's Lament")

–ong rhymes (as in gong)

gong	throng
prong	tong
thong	

–ood rhymes (also –ould)

could   should   would
good   stood
hood   wood

Some harder words: boxwood, childhood, firewood, likelihood, neighborhood, rosewood, understood

A terrible thing about grammar,
It raises a terrible clamor,
Is when to use **could***,*
And when to use **would***,*
Or **should** *it be* **should**
When **would** *is no* **good***?*
It's enough to make a kid stammer.

–ood rhymes (also –eud; –ude)_____

brood	feud	mood	shrewd
crude	food	nude	
dude	lewd	rude	

Some harder words: attitude, conclude, delude, elude, exclude, include, interlude, intrude, prelude, rood, seclude, snood

Timely tip: You can make other **–ood** rhymes by adding **–ed** to words ending in **–oo**, **–ue**, and **–ew**, like **booed**, **glued**, and **stewed**.

–ook rhymes_____

book	crook	nook
brook	hook	shook
cook	look	took

Some harder words: buttonhook, fishhook, mistook, pocketbook, scrapbook, textbook, unhook

–ool rhymes (also –oul; –uel; –ule)

cool	duel	ghoul	rule	stool
cruel	fool	gruel	school	tool
drool	fuel	pool	spool	yule

Some harder words: footstool, granule, toadstool, module, molecule, pule, ridicule, vestibule, whirlpool

*Joe Chipmunk thought he was **cool**,*
*By skipping his homework for **school**.*
"Do homework? No way,"
He was proud to say,
*But by midterm he looked like a **fool**.*

–oom rhymes (also –omb; –ume)_____

boom	gloom	plume	womb
broom	groom	room	zoom
doom	loom	tomb	
fume			

Some harder words: assume, bridegroom, broadloom, consume, mushroom, perfume, resume

–oon rhymes (also –ewn; –une)_____

boon	hewn	soon	swoon
coon	noon	spoon	tune
croon	prune	strewn	
dune			

Some harder words: afternoon, baboon, balloon, bassoon, harpoon, honeymoon, lagoon, macaroon, maroon, monsoon, raccoon, saloon, teaspoon

Heigh, diddle diddle, the cat and the fiddle,
The cow jumped over the **moon**.
The little dog laughed to see such sport,
And the dish ran away with the **spoon**.
—Nursery Rhyme

–oop rhymes (also –oup; –oupe; –upe)_____

coop	dupe	poop	soup	troupe
coupe	group	scoop	stoop	whoop
croup	hoop	sloop	swoop	
droop	loop	snoop	troop	

–ooper rhymes (also –ouper; –uper; –upor)

blooper	looper	stupor	trouper
cooper	scooper	super	
grouper	snooper	trooper	

*The Cy Young Award to the **grouper**.*
*Day in and day out, he's a **trouper**.*
When he pitches the ball,
It's three strikes, that's all,
*And the batters swim off in a **stupor**.*

–oor rhymes (also –eur; –our; –ure)_____

boor	moor	sure
cure	poor	tour
lure	pure	

Some harder words: allure, amateur, assure, contour, demure, detour, endure, gravure, insure, obscure, spoor

–oose rhymes (also –uce; –use)_____

deuce	moose	truce
goose	noose	use
loose	spruce	

Some harder words: caboose, excuse, induce, mongoose, papoose, produce, puce, reduce, reproduce

–oot rhymes (also –uit; –ute)_____

boot	flute	lute	route	suit
brute	fruit	moot	scoot	toot
chute	hoot	newt	shoot	
coot	loot	root	snoot	

Some harder words: astute, commute, compute, dilute, dispute, parachute, persecute, pollute, pursuit, recruit, repute, salute, tribute

–op rhymes (also –ap)

bop	drop	lop	prop	stop
chop	flop	mop	shop	strop
crop	fop	plop	slop	swap
cop	hop	pop	sop	top

Some harder words: eavesdrop, gumdrop, pawn-shop, raindrop, shortstop, teardrop, workshop

–ope rhymes (also –oap)

cope	hope	pope	slope
dope	lope	rope	soap
grope	mope	scope	

Some harder words: antelope, elope, envelope, gyroscope, horoscope, kaleidoscope, periscope, telescope

–opper rhymes (also –oper)

bopper	dropper	proper	topper
chopper	hopper	shopper	whopper
copper	popper	stopper	

–ore rhymes (also –oar; –oor; –or; –our)

boar	fore	oar	score	store
core	four	or	shore	swore
chore	gore	ore	snore	tore
door	lore	pore	soar	wore
floor	more	pour	sore	yore
for	nor	roar	spore	your

Some harder words: abhor, adore, before, deplore, dinosaur, encore, explore, futhermore, galore, hoar, ignore, indoor, pinafore, restore, sophomore, sycamore, tor, troubadour

> *When I was down beside the sea,*
> *A wooden spade they gave me*
> *   To dig the sandy* **shore.**
> *My holes were empty like a cup,*
> *In every hole the sea came up,*
> *   Till it could come no* **more.**
> —Robert Louis Stevenson
> ("At the Seaside")

–orn rhymes (also –arn; –ourn)_____

born	morn	shorn	torn
corn	mourn	sworn	warn
horn	scorn	thorn	worn

Some harder words: acorn, adorn, foghorn, hawthorn, popcorn, unicorn

This is the farmer sowing the **corn**,
That kept the cock that crowed in the **morn**,
That waked the priest all shaven and **shorn**,
That married the man all tattered and **torn**,
That kissed the maiden all **forlorn**,
That milked the cow with the crumpled **horn**,
That tossed the dog
That worried the cat
That killed the rat
That ate the malt
That lay in the house that Jack built.

— Nursery Rhyme

–ort rhymes (also –art; –ourt)_____

court	quart	sort
fort	short	thwart
port	snort	wart

Some harder words: abort, assort, cavort, contort, deport, escort, export, extort, import, passport, report, resort, retort, seaport, support, tort, transport

–ose rhymes (also –oze) _____

chose	doze	hose	pose	rose
close	froze	nose	prose	those

Some harder words: arose, compose, disclose, dispose, expose, foreclose, oppose, primrose, propose

Timely tip: Don't forget all those plural words which could be used here—like **blows**, **clothes**, **goes**, **toes**.

–oss rhymes (also –auce) _____

boss	floss	moss
cross	gloss	sauce
dross	loss	toss

> *"Ride a cockhorse to Banbury **Cross**"*
> *Is not my idea of a very good rhyme.*
> *For **cross** rhymes with **hoss***
> *And not horse of course.*
> *Methinks this is less than sublime.*

–ot rhymes (also –acht; –at; –att)_____

blot	hot	not	slot	trot
cot	jot	plot	spot	watt
dot	knot	pot	squat	what
got	lot	shot	swat	yacht

Some harder words: allot, ascot, boycott, forgot, foxtrot, jackpot, mascot, slingshot, snapshot, teapot, upshot

*Pease-porridge **hot**,*
Pease-porridge cold,
*Pease-porridge in the **pot**,*
Nine days old.
 —Nursery Rhyme

–otter rhymes (also –atter)

cotter	potter	squatter
hotter	plotter	swatter
otter	spotter	totter

–ound rhymes

bound	hound	round
found	mound	sound
ground	pound	wound

Some harder words: around, astound, background, compound, greyhound, playground, profound, rebound, resound, spellbound, surround

Timely tip: Check the rhymes under **–own** for words to which you can add **–ed**, like **frowned**.

–ounder rhymes

bounder	grounder	sounder
flounder	pounder	
founder	rounder	

*The double play fish is the **flounder**.*
*At shortstop no fish is **sounder**.*
When push comes to shove
And he puts on his glove,
*He is peerless at fielding a **grounder**.*

–our rhymes (also –ower)

bower	flower	power	sour
cower	hour	scour	tower
flour	our	shower	

–ouse rhymes

blouse	house	spouse
douse	louse	
grouse	mouse	

> There was a crooked man, and he went a crooked
> mile,
> He found a crooked sixpence against a crooked
> stile.
> He bought a crooked cat, which caught a crooked
> **mouse**,
> And they all lived together in a little crooked
> **house**.
>
> —Nursery Rhyme

–out rhymes (also –oubt)

bout	gout	rout	spout	trout
doubt	lout	scout	sprout	
drought	out	shout	stout	
flout	pout	snout	tout	

Some harder words: about, devout, layout, lookout, throughout, without

> *For speed on the diamond the **trout**.*
> *Once on base he's never put **out**.*
> *When he slides into home*
> *In a whirlpool of foam,*
> *He is safe by the length of his **snout**.*

–ow rhymes (also –ou; –ough)

bough	brow	meow	plough	vow
bow	cow	now	scow	wow
bow-wow	how	plow	thou	

Some harder words: allow, anyhow, avow, endow, eyebrow, somehow

> *I never saw a purple **cow**,*
> *I never hope to see one.*
> *But I can tell you **anyhow**,*
> *I'd rather see than be one.*
> —Gelett Burgess
> ("The Purple Cow")

–owl rhymes (also –oul; –owel)

bowel	foul	howl	prowl	trowel
cowl	fowl	jowl	scowl	vowel
dowel	growl	owl	towel	

*Don't call an **owl***
*A **fowl**.*
*A **fowl** can't hoot,*
*An **owl** can't scoot,*
*And the **owl** is likely to **scowl**!*

–own rhymes (also –oun)

brown	down	gown
clown	drown	noun
crown	frown	town

Some harder words: downtown, letdown, nightgown, renown, showdown, uptown

The lion and the unicorn
Were fighting for the **crown**.
The lion beat the unicorn
All around the **town**.
Some gave them white bread,
And some gave them **brown**;
Some gave them plum cake
And sent them out of **town**.
—Nursery Rhyme

–ox rhymes

box	ox
fox	phlox
lox	pox

Some harder words: chatterbox, equinox, ortho-dox, paradox, smallpox, soapbox, strongbox

Timely tip: If you need more, make plurals out of words ending in **–ock**, like **docks** and **socks**.

–oy rhymes (also –oi)

boy	poi
coy	toy
joy	

Some harder words: ahoy, alloy, annoy, corduroy, decoy, destroy, employ, enjoy, playboy

–ub rhymes

club	flub	nub	scrub	stub
cub	grub	pub	shrub	sub
dub	hub	rub	snub	tub

–uch rhymes (also –ouch; –utch)

clutch	hutch	touch
crutch	much	
dutch	such	

–uck rhymes

buck	duck	pluck	struck	tuck
chuck	luck	puck	stuck	truck
cluck	muck	shuck	suck	

Some harder words: amok, awestruck, moonstruck, potluck, ruek, sawbuck, woodchuck

–ud rhymes (also –ood)

blood	dud	spud
bud	flood	stud
cud	mud	thud

–udge rhymes

budge	grudge	sludge
drudge	judge	smudge
fudge	nudge	trudge

Which is better:
*Bearing a **grudge***
*Or eating chocolate **fudge**?*
Which is better?
*You be the **judge**!*

–uff rhymes (also –ough)

bluff	fluff	muff	scruff	tough
buff	gruff	puff	scuff	
cuff	huff	rough	snuff	
duff	luff	ruff	stuff	

Some harder words: dandruff, enough, handcuff, rebuff, slough

–ug rhymes

bug	hug	plug	slug	tug
chug	jug	pug	smug	
drug	lug	rug	snug	
dug	mug	shrug	thug	

Snug
As a **bug**
In a **rug**.

—Benjamin Franklin
(from a letter to Miss Georgiana Shipley)

–ull rhymes (as in dull)_____

cull	hull	scull
dull	lull	skull
gull	mull	

Be careful! There are two groups of words ending in **–ull** which look alike but don't sound alike. You have to say a word out loud to make sure which group it belongs to.

–ull rhymes (as in bull; also –ool)_____

bull	wool
full	
pull	

–um rhymes (also –ome; –umb) _____

bum	drum	hum	plumb	slum
chum	dumb	mum	rum	some
come	glum	numb	scrum	sum
crumb	gum	plum	scum	thumb

*"Why so **glum**?"*
*Asked the fingers of the **thumb**.*
"What could be so bad
As to make you look so sad?"
*"I'm not **glum**,"*
*Said the **thumb** in reply,*
*"But the elbow called me **dumb***
And I have no alibi."

–umble rhymes _____

bumble	grumble	mumble	tumble
crumble	humble	rumble	
fumble	jumble	stumble	

*Bees **bumble**,*
*Cookies **crumble**,*
*Footballs **fumble**,*
*Grouches **grumble**,*
*Towers **tumble**.*
But can you tell us, my good friend,
*Who can **jumble**?*
*Who can **mumble**?*
*Who can **rumble**?*
*Who can **stumble**?*

–ump rhymes

bump	dump	jump	pump	stump
chump	frump	lump	rump	thump
clump	hump	plump	slump	trump

*From the stairs I hear a **clump**,*
*Near my bed a telltale **thump**.*
*Nothing else can make me **jump***
*Like things in the night that go **bump**.*

–un rhymes (also –on; –one)

bun	gun	one	shun	sun
done	none	pun	son	ton
fun	nun	run	spun	won

Some harder words: begun, canyon, dun, homespun, rhododendron, shotgun, someone

Tom, Tom, the piper's **son**,
Stole a pig and away he **run**.
The pig was eat, and Tom was beat,
And Tom went howling down the street.
—Nursery Rhyme

–ung rhymes (also –ongue)

clung	hung	slung	sung	wrung
dung	lung	strung	swung	young
flung	rung	stung	tongue	

Some harder words: among, bung, farflung, high-strung, unsung

–unk rhymes (also –onk)

bunk	drunk	hunk	punk	stunk
chunk	flunk	junk	skunk	sunk
clunk	funk	monk	slunk	trunk
dunk	gunk	plunk	spunk	

–unny rhymes (also –oney)

bunny	honey
funny	money
gunny	sunny

> *One for the **money**,*
> *Two for the dough,*
> *Three for bread and **honey**,*
> *And away we go!*

–unt rhymes (also –ont)

blunt	front	runt
brunt	hunt	shunt
bunt	punt	stunt

–ur rhymes (also –er; –ere; –ir; –irr; –urr)

blur	fir	purr	slur	were
burr	fur	sir	spur	whirr
cur	her	shirr	stir	

Some harder words: bestir, concur, confer, defer, demur, incur, myrrh, occur, recur, refer

Be careful! There are many more words ending in –er which *might* be added to this list, like **mother**, **teacher**, etc., but we've chosen not to because they don't quite rhyme. Say them out loud, compare them to, say, **fur** or **stir**, and you'll hear the difference.

*Oh I wish I **were**, I wish I **were**,*
A-riding on my steed.
*Then I'd say to me, "Good morning, **sir**,*
A fine day, yes indeed!"

–url rhymes (also –earl; –erle; –irl; –orl)

churl	furl	pearl	twirl
curl	girl	purl	whirl
earl	hurl	swirl	whorl

Who would be
A mermaid fair,
Singing alone,
Combing her hair
Under the sea,
In a golden **curl**
With a comb of **pearl**,
On a throne?
—Alfred, Lord Tennyson
("The Mermaid")

–urn rhymes (also –earn; –ern)_____

burn	fern	stern	urn
churn	learn	tern	yearn
earn	spurn	turn	

Some harder words: adjourn, auburn, cistern, concern, discern, erne, intern, return, sojourn, taciturn

–urry rhymes (also –orry)_____

blurry	furry	worry
curry	hurry	
flurry	scurry	

–us rhymes (also –ous; –uss)_____

bus	muss	thus
cuss	plus	truss
fuss	pus	

Some harder words: discuss, surplus, unanimous

–ush rhymes_____

blush	flush	lush	slush
brush	gush	plush	thrush
crush	hush	rush	

Be careful! Bush and **push** look as though they belong in this list, but they really don't. Say them out loud and hear the difference.

*When o'er the world there falls a **hush**,*
*And over too the long day's **rush**,*
Then children in their beds will sleep
While I, who cannot, count my sheep
*All through the night, till dawn's first **blush**.*

–ust rhymes

bust	gust	must	trust
crust	just	rust	
dust	lust	thrust	

Some harder words: adjust, august, disgust, distrust, entrust, robust, unjust

Timely tip: In addition, there are the –us and –uss rhymes to which an –ed can be added, like **bussed** and **mussed**.

–ut rhymes (also –utt)

but	glut	mutt	rut	strut
butt	hut	nut	shut	
cut	jut	putt	smut	

Some harder words: abut, chestnut, cocoanut, doughnut, halibut, peanut, walnut

–utter rhymes

butter	flutter	putter	stutter
clutter	gutter	shutter	strutter
cutter	mutter	sputter	utter

–y rhymes (also –eye; –i; –ie; –igh; –uy; –ye)

aye	fie	lye	sigh	tie
by	fly	my	sky	try
buy	fry	nigh	sly	vie
cry	guy	pie	spry	why
die	hie	ply	spy	wry
dry	high	pry	sty	
dye	I	rye	thigh	
eye	lie	shy	thy	

Some harder words: alibi, ally, alumni, apply, awry, deny, defy, firefly, hereby, imply, lullaby, mortify, multiply, nearby, occupy, pi, rabbi, rely, reply, satisfy, supply

> *O little town of Bethlehem!*
> *How still we see thee **lie**.*
> *Above thy deep and dreamless sleep*
> *The silent stars go **by**.*
>
> —Phillips Brooks
> ("O Little Town of Bethlehem")

Index

Rhymes and Sounds

E

O

U

Y